THE BODIES
OF BIRDS

THE BODIES
OF BIRDS

MELANIE RAE THON

NEW MICHIGAN PRESS

TUCSON, ARIZONA

NEW MICHIGAN PRESS

DEPT OF ENGLISH, P. O. BOX 210067

UNIVERSITY OF ARIZONA

TUCSON, AZ 85721-0067

<http://newmichiganpress.com>

Orders and queries to <nmp@thediagram.com>.

ISBN 978-1-934832-68-4. FIRST PRINTING.

Printed in the United States of America.

Design by Ander Monson.

Cover photograph by Dennis Kirkland
https://www.denniskirkland.com/

CONTENTS

In the Exclusion Zone   I

The Bodies of Birds   15

Requiem in the Rain   35

Acknowledgments   49

For our beloved ones, human and more than human,
who through their beautiful bodies keep us alive,
and sustain us, and deliver us whole moment by moment—

IN THE EXCLUSION ZONE

Twenty-seven years, and in the utter
absence of human life, in the stunned
silence of human voices,
red deer and fierce boar
flourish—in the Exclusion Zone,
in Chernobyl's Zone of Alienation,
the wolf, the lynx, the bear find refuge.

Foxes, polecats, wild horses.
The beaver returns, restores
the marshes. Bison roam the woods.
Bees make glowing honey.

Over the scorched throat
of the reactor, above
but not-so-far beyond
the sarcophagus
hiding the hot heart
of Chernobyl, home

into the primeval oaks
of the Forbidden Zone,

black storks glide, white bellies
exposed, red beaks flashing.

No human eye to see: a cloud
of birds, a shadow crossing

the earth—and then: light
through leaves—

scattered light everywhere.

*Four hundred thousand humans gone—everything gone—cats,
dogs, air to breathe, hungry cattle—our father's wheat, our
mother's chickens—gone, the horse we loved—fields of grass,
early morning—he carried us on his swayed back. The day the
day didn't come, we heard the blast of our father's rifle, felt bone
pierce brain as our father shot him.*

Home, too dangerous to go there—
twenty-seven years, the earth still hot
with radiation. Dolls lie
in the dust, faces pocked, arms
twisted—a world of glass,
windowpanes in shards, china
shattered—birds roost
in your broken home,

thrive in the peace of your open
spaces—birds line their nests
with lace and grass, human hair,
faces, family—
photographs torn by rain,
words of love, letters tattered.

In the Zone of Alienation, saplings
sprout from the kitchen floor,
willows grow through broken windows—

vines climb up the walls
to tear them down later.

Wild grape, feral roses—rain
rots wood to pluck
strings of your piano.

The curved back of the cello
splits and peels, splinters
down the long spine,

sings to itself in the rain, cracks
in the sun, after.

The owl returns from a night's work,
disgorges bones bound
with hair and feathers—

the bear has found your bed unmade,
your doors and roof forever open.

*To ourselves and others, we were known not as Pelia, Vassia,
Viktor, Volodya—not Tolik, Eduard, Igor, Gregori—not
as seven hundred thousand separate souls, but as one, as
liquidators.*

*In the beginning, we were on the roof of Reactor Three, heaving
shovels full of debris into the heart of the fire. Ninety seconds
was a lifetime's work, a thousand years of radiation.*

*For the sacrifice of our bodies, we received medals with drops
of blood and the signs we now know as our own, particles and
rays—Alpha, Beta, Gamma—we were radioactive waste,
heroes of the state, dangerous to wives and doctors, children in
the womb, children not imagined. We offered our bodies inside
and out. Some of us died fast, and some refused to die and
didn't. Our bodies were secrets of the state—skin burned black,
flesh crackling—our lungs came out our mouths—our hearts,*

our livers—our bowels dissolved—our tongues split in our mouths—our mouths peeled off in layers.

If we were among the lucky, blessed enough to die, they buried us in wood and zinc, lead and plastic. Twenty-seven years and even now our bodies glow underground. Even now our hair could kill you.

> *Dangerous, the dead—*
> *our radioactive bodies speak*
> *their own language.*

Not Vladimir, Alyosha, Sergei, Gennady—not Valentin, Ivan, Nicolai, Dimitri—we were one, we came after—after rain, after fire—after the humans were gone, four hundred thousand gone—removed, evacuated, gone—forbidden to return because here, on this earth, the soil is dangerous—the hair of your cat, the bones of your terrier—mushrooms bloom in the brain—the geraniums, the berries—the dust on the leaves destroys the throat as you breathe it.

> *Everything will kill, everything poison.*
> *Everything you love we came to bury.*

We buried the earth, cut into the soil and rolled the earth like a rug—grass, flowers, worms, beetles—heaved the earth into shallow graves, buried the earth with ants and spiders. We sawed trees and buried forests—eggs, milk, wells, gardens. You left a note on the door:

> *Please don't hurt the cat.*
> *She kills the voles. She helps*
> *the garden. Dear, kind Person,*
> *Use whatever you need,*
> *but please, don't trash the house.*
> *We'll be home soon.*
> *We'll come home later.*

We dug a pit on the side of your house. We buried your house in the pit. We buried your village.

You can't come home to the Zone. The Zone is off limits. We photographed ourselves in your vacant houses. We ate the canned beans. We ate the canned cherries.

> *Dear, kind Person,*
> *Use whatever you need.*

We shot your cats and dogs. Their fur, their breath, their tongues—dangerous.

Why speak now? The human mind is not enough to understand it.

Before we came, your dogs and cats ate eggs, then chickens—cucumbers, tomatoes—then the dogs ate the cats, and the cats ate their babies. We came to save. We came to deliver. The horse knew everything. The white horse cried when we took him to the field.

Some of us liked to kill, and some were sick after. We drank vodka to kill, and vodka to protect us from radiation. In the beginning your dogs ran toward us, but later they growled and charged. They showed us their terrible teeth, and we had to kill your dogs because everything you love grows feral.

The apple tree bloomed. The lilac flowered—rose, jasmine, poppy, lily—everything alive, but strange—the day blue and still, but we couldn't smell the blossoms. We worked twelve-hour shifts. We gave our blood. We drank your vodka. We killed everything that moved, and then everything that didn't. And then one day we were standing in the forest, and we saw a hundred ants on a single branch, ten thousand on one slender

birch tree. We saw spiders and worms, all going their way,
each with some purpose. We didn't know their names. We
didn't know their children. We were seven hundred thousand
beings, so many human beings, and still our human lives meant
nothing. We began to understand the infinities of lives lost, the
ones we killed, the ones we buried. If you learn to love this way,
the whole world destroys you.

Four hundred thousand humans gone, evacuated from the Zone,
forbidden to return to their radioactive farms, their dangerous
gardens. In the villages we didn't bury, the weight of snow
collapsed roofs, fire tore through splintered rafters. We thought
nothing could survive. The bones of animals would bear no
weight; the eggs of birds would crack and crumble. Sterile or
mutant, everything strange, but no one told the storks, and no
one told the weasels. They loved this new world, the earth wet
without humans.

Beavers appeared by the hundreds and thousands. They
worked day after day, damming man-made canals, tunneling
under dikes, restoring marshes for frogs and moose, egrets and
cormorants—mosquitoes, gnats, otters, turtles—returning farms
to wilderness faster than any human dared imagine—decades
of work undone—and soon the fox returned to hunt vole and
rabbit. Bear and badger came—eagle, falcon. The boar grew fat,
too fat to kill, and wolves returned but feared to stalk him.

Snow melted in the Carpathian Mountains and flowed four hundred miles northeast to flood abandoned fields. Without canals or dikes to slow the water, the Pripyat River rose twenty-five feet and spread ten miles. And the beaver saw that it was good, and with his holy work continued.

In the Exclusion Zone, time spins backward. In the Zone of Alienation, bison return to the forest—black storks, wild horses. We did not imagine these beings. The human mind did not invent them.

Days after the fires of Chernobyl, as whirling winds carried radioactive particles to Poland, Germany, Austria, Romania—Switzerland, France, Belgium, India—England, Greece, Israel, Canada—Kuwait, Japan, Turkey, America—as radioactive rain fell on Waterford, Ireland—as thousands of poisoned reindeer in Scandinavia were oh-so-mercifully slaughtered and buried, the people of this planet learned: every particle of rain touches the face; everyone on earth is ours; anything on earth can happen.

Home, twenty-seven years and still so dangerous, but they come, refugees and recalcitrants, because they are less afraid of poisoned earth than poisoned cities, because they are safer in Belarus than they were in Tajikistan, Uzbekistan, Kyrgyzstan, the Caucasus.

Because strontium and cesium and plutonium
are invisible, and the guns of the soldiers

where we once lived, the spit and curse
of neighbors in Minsk and Kiev, the smoke
of fires and fumes of cars

in Moscow, the rocks of children—
these things we see. These things are real.

And look, there are houses here, collapsing,
yes, but we can fix them. The earth bestows.

Who can be afraid of roses
and raspberries?
Tell us, please: who can fear soil
and water, beets and squash—
apples, pears—
mushrooms, potatoes?

The cow looks thin, yes, but offers her body, shares
with us warm milk every morning.

Eat, here, please, sit with us
tonight, taste one sweet red tomato.

If our bodies feel strange, we call it joy. If our cells
feel full of light, we believe we are transfigured.

> *Let your dosimeters spin and beep.*
> *What can numbers tell you? The eagle*
> *eats the carp and flies so high above us.*

> *Egret, owl, partridge, warbler—if falcons*
> *don't fear voles, why should we refuse*
> *the wheat, the cream, the glowing honey?*

Yes, we know, the sarcophagus is cracking—yes,
we hear you: the hot heart of Chernobyl burns beneath it.

We know not how it hurts, but we can promise you this:
when the heart explodes again, we'll need no words:

> *the wind and the rain will tell us.*

Listen: we promise: every body dies: blood and breath,
the same: and when we do, we die like animals.

THE BODIES OF BIRDS

The light of late afternoon touching everything—my
hands, my face, the wings of birds—illuminating edges of
clouds—the kitchen a bottle of light, pale green filling with
sound—the woman playing piano in a room down the
hall—everything clean until the boy, the girl, the husband
come home—I'm on my knees in the light scrubbing the
floor—my hands glow, cells trembling, body swollen with
sound, heart stunned, and suddenly wounded—notes so fast
and low they pulse down the hall through the floor rising
from me—

                                                    I am
forbidden to touch the piano—except to dust, unless to
polish—but here it is, tremors of light, voices shimmering—
she can't stop birds or clouds, light becoming sound, outside
coming in, sound becoming body—

My father waits behind hedges at the back of the house—
he's been persuaded not to knock at the door, not to rush
or distract me—I feel him now, hot in the blue Dodge,
windows closed, radio throbbing—he's been warned not
to let his music pulse into the house—those guitars, those
voices—my brother Benito's body quivers with sound—
tendons struck, bones buzzing—syncopations jolt his
heart—he's hot, he's hungry—Benito strapped in the back,
diaper damp, fist shoved hard against his teeth to keep from
wailing—

                                                    My father cares nothing
for the woman's peace, her time, the light, her piano, this
hour—he's been severing limbs since dawn, hacking bone,
slicing muscle—nine hours splattered in blood—he hosed
himself down at work, but he carries the smell on his breath,
in his mind, in his hair, on his fingers—everywhere he goes,
the bodies of animals, the chests he cleaved, God, his own
chest open, ribs split wide, bowels untangling—he saw
heads in a heap, three men cutting tongues, slabs of tongue
tossed on a table—what he wants now is a dark room, water
so hot it burns, a sound fierce and fast enough to scorch
memory—

Bodies waver at the edge of the woods, deer waiting till dusk to surge into the woman's yard, strip the roses—those heads, those blossoms—soon to be the flesh of deer, dark dreams of themselves, animals leaping—

Clouds swell, and in this loss of light, shapes become human, men dressed as deer, hands raised above their heads, fingers curved to cast the shadows of antlers—women with glittering eyes, owls carrying children—they ran, they flew—days and years, hundreds of miles—hot wind cracked their skin, their bones broke, their blood congealed—they fell down dead in a ditch, drank dirt and swallowed—they crawled to the Rio Bravo—whirling silt, sweet water—half humans so thirsty they believed they could drink the river and walk—now here they are—they almost made it—

I know them—I see them everywhere—picking jalapeños and pecans, hauling trash, washing windows—I see them mowing lawns, tanks of gasoline strapped to their backs— they spark and spin, burst to flame, explode in your mind, in your yard as you watch them—

I know it is a mistake to call the light tender, but not wrong
now to feel its indiscriminate love touching my mouth,
the bones of my ears, my heart, my fingers—I remember
clouds opened, and the music stopped—the long shadows
of pine spread across the lawn—five crows walked between
them—I slipped out of the house and into the car, kissed my
father's face, pulled my brother's fingers from his mouth—

                              They wanted none of me, nothing
kind, nothing human—and then we were driving home,
dusk, almost home, fifteen miles—I turned the radio off,
tried to find the woman's music, follow notes down my spine,
remember sound through my pelvis—

If it's true what they say—so much space between cells, so
much space inside atoms—why can't the spaces of me slip
through glass, fast as light, slip through metal—

I know it's possible—a girl stabbed in the heart
doesn't die—a baby dropped five floors doesn't
shatter—somebody wants them to die, but no, they
won't—no, they didn't—

The skin of a sixteen-year-old girl
regenerates every twenty-two days—down
the throat, through the colon—inside
and out, so little difference—continuous,
miraculous, my skin protecting even now the
open wounds of a burned child—

                    Weeks or days—soon
enough his body will reject mine—but now,
tonight, as the drugged boy drifts through
dreams he won't remember—*birds falling
from the sky, howling dogs, fur on fire*—
tonight, the collagen of my skin fuses into
the scraped clean, scoured pits where once
there was blood and muscle—

Now we are
one, now we
are quiet—
in the dream
we share I am
unwinding
bandages to
reveal our
spectacular
body, veins
visible, skin
new and fine
as the skin
of a fetus—

You read about us in the paper: *Boy Torched by Bike Thieves,
Girl Killed in Crash Donates Organs*—thirty-seven days and
hundreds of miles between us, but here we are, safe and still,
becoming one, the same body—

                                             I surrendered all I knew—heart and
lungs, discs of the vertebrae, the dark secret of my spleen,
unscarred skin—corneas, pancreas, the delicate bones of my
ears, my impossible love, all I had to give—kidneys, liver,
veins, cartilage—I offered the gloriously pliable tissue of
my thighs, a song moving through the spaces between cells,
consciousness unstrung, bowels unspooled—continuous,
miraculous, the bodies I am tonight, uncontained by
multitudes—

As a child not so long ago I found the skull of a fox, femur,
pelvis—skin of a black snake—ribcage of a feral cat, bones
of a bird's wing nested inside it—

I remember dusk darkening the spaces between trees, a
murmuration of birds—a funnel, a storm—thousands
of bodies flying as one—starlings swooping low over a
fallow field, black earth cleaved—the smell of dirt, my
father's window open wide, cold wind rushing through
us—I remember my brother's whimper and wailing cry,
unbuckling my seatbelt to turn and soothe him—

My father swerved into the left lane
but didn't pass the car beside us—I saw you, a man alone,
I remember how long we stared, some kind of terrible love,
dark birds whirling between us—my father said, *Let him cry,*
buckle your belt, leave him—

I was afraid of my father—spatters of blood on his boots,
pigs crying in a kill pit—their flesh, their fat, their long
bodies—their miraculous minds—afraid to imagine soft
ears, curled tails—pink skin and dark eyes—their curious
gaze, before and after—

Shush, it's okay, we're okay, almost home now—

Afraid to disobey, yes, but I did not turn from you or my
brother—*shush, Benito, no*—my brother sobbed so hard my
chest hurt, and you read my lips, or heard me—

Impossible I know,
but I still believe you saw everything inside, you knew us as
dusk became dark, as birds vanished—my father hit the gas
hard—angry with you or me or the baby or the pig—the
birds, the field, the smell of dirt, the dead, the shadows
between trees—*you fell far behind, and I thought, there, it's
done, I've lost you*—

Benito only sputtered now, too tired to wail, and I did begin
to turn in time to see blue light fill the car—but not in time
to sit, pull the strap tight, snap the buckle—

You see us on the nightly news—seven car crash caused by
two girls cranked on Benzedrine, numb with tequila—wind
whipping their hair, half sisters in flight, a game of Truth or
Dare, the silver Lexus stolen from their father—wailing into
the wind, runaway children blasting down the wrong side of
the road, 80 miles per hour—

You know me,
the one lifted in a helicopter—alive, yes, but extremely
critical—meaning my head slammed into the roof before my
body flew into the windshield, meaning ejected as the car
rolled, flung into the ditch as the door popped open—

Anika Vela, the name withheld, unknown, unspoken—
pending notification of relatives—my mother and three
sisters, my cousins, my uncle—my blind grandmother who
swam the Rio Bravo with my father no bigger than Benito
clinging to her back, who saw her own sister swept away,
swirling down the murky river—my grandmother who had
to choose sister or son, who swam hard to the other shore,
who let her go, who did not save her—Marielena who chose
my father and me, the beating heart against her skin, the
ones unborn, the lives imagined—

No, not Anika, not possible—

Marielena didn't survive for this, to bury me before her—

You won't see them on the news—my mother, my father—
in a small room with one window where they have been
told, where a doctor has carefully articulated the damage
to the skull, the brain, the stem, the cortex—where he has
explained the fixed eye, dilation of the pupil, the ventilator
they use to keep the body oxygenated, the medications
without which my blood pressure will plunge, my heart
stutter and fail—

Now the man is gone and God
here is my father's reflection in dark glass—one terrible
blind eye, the face dissolved—he is pounding his head on
the glass and it hurts or it must hurt, but he can't stop—

As a child my mother prayed to see the face of God—now,
face to face, Tereza Vela turns the light off—

The sun will rise and go down, the flesh be
cleaved, the body opened—human hands will
hold the human heart—the lungs, the liver—
meteors will pummel the earth, cold rain pound
the desert—the body of one will be many—
ditches will flood and spill, rivers surge and
roil—some of the bodies will swirl in silt, some
gasp and breathe, some swim to shore—

And my father will lie
in the dark, listening
to blood, listening to water—
hearing the heart, the rain,
the stem, the cortex—
Mateo Vela will go out
in the light to hold the rib,
to touch the pelvis—
to be one, to be nothing—
to disappear
with the disappeared—
breath and dirt, skin
of the snake, skull
of the rabbit—

There are things you see but can't believe—flames in the street, flames whirling toward your house in the shape of a child—

((*and a woman wearing a mask is stitching the cornea to your eye with sutures finer than the hair of a baby*))

You are wrapping the burning boy in a blanket, pulling the hose straight to spray the body with water—

((*and a man dressed as a doctor is slipping bones in your ear, a kidney in your pelvis*))

You hear howling dogs and you open your eyes in the dark to see what you don't see—birds falling from the sky, your burned hand, the scorched blanket—

Sometimes you are afraid of the heart, the vagus nerve cut, the heart beating too fast always—last summer, waiting for the heart, you almost died of a bee sting—in January, the flu—in March, pneumonia—your lungs filled, your kidneys failed—you died and returned—your swollen, failing heart fluttering inside you—

((*and the woman wearing a mask whispers a needle into your vein: shush, it's okay, we're okay, almost home now*))

You are asleep and awake, fully conscious, eyes closed but able to see through closed eyelids, and a girl with long dark hair is opening your body with the sharp blades of her hands—the one whose face you never dared imagine is singing her way through your bones, speaking your name to the dark as she sews the bodies of trembling birds into your trembling body—

REQUIEM IN THE RAIN

Blessed are the ones who surrender,
who ask not why, who do what is needed.

In a prison in California, a man who killed a woman a hundred times, who stabbed face and throat, heart and belly, who soaked himself in blood and rendered the body beneath his own unrecognizable, now washes another man in the shower, shaves his face, changes his diapers, protects and serves a murderer like himself, riddled by dementia— *blood everywhere, her eyes in my hands, she called me sweet heart*—knows repentance not as the hour of remorse, but as patience, surrender, a lifetime's work, the choice, the freedom, now, turning toward love every moment.

> *Brother, no one on this earth is unworthy of forgiveness*
>   *(killed her a hundred times)*
>
> *no matter what you've done, there is a path, love*
>   *(rendered the body)*
>
> *a way to become, to return to the self*
>   *(eyes, hands, heart) to be human.*

*I dream you in a place like this, a sanctuary, a prison, alive all
these years, not wounded by a state trooper, not bleeding out
in a nest of rags and leaves under the freeway—sweet brother,
given back this choice, this freedom, offered the gift, the blessing
of purpose—I see you bathing a man old and forgetful as our
father, standing with him beneath a sharp spray of water,
thanking him, washing his withered flesh, safe and saved,
thanking the water, each of you unafraid, each in his own way
healed—the beatitudes inscribed—not as words, but as actions.*

Every body dies, yes, and when we do, we die like animals.

Gabriel, my brother, in the surveillance video I see him shot
twice robbing a convenience store, willing to kill a girl, a
child, a stranger he might have loved—my brother willing to
die for two hundred dollars. The blast through the jaw feels
like the whole head exploding. Everything dissipates in fog,
gone, into a vast cloud of unknowing.

*Dear Brother, I dream time spinning backward, you and the
girl behind the counter face to face, seeing each other as you are,
close enough to smell, to taste the damp air between you, two
transient beings, trembling. We hear the tiny Beretta snap, feel
the heat in our hands, and already it is too late, already the past
past, the future now, every moment.*

Blessed are the poor in spirit, the ones
who have and want and are nothing.

There are a billion cells in the heart, thirty billion ion channels. Every moment of her beautiful life each one has worked perfectly. We feel again the crack of the gun, but look, she's not falling; she's unfolding, rising up from the floor, and the bullet leaves her throat and returns to the pistol—the video whorls in reverse, and my brother slips the gun in the pocket, and the girl, *my God*, this time he sees her—pale skin and teeth so perfect—she's not afraid: she's almost smiling—and he's not going to do this thing—*no*, he's winding backward down the aisles, unwalking a bright labyrinth, stepping lightly into fog where the cloud of fog receives him.

But you have killed, now and forever she will die, and the
trooper has wounded you, forever now you are dying.

Blessed are the poor in spirit, the ones
who have and want and are nothing.

Thirty billion ion channels and now not one sparks the heart. Now not even God can save us.

My brother has found his way home, has plunged through fog, holding the shattered jaw with one hand, as if the hand can contain him. He stumbles on tangled roots, falls and surrenders. Rats smell his blood, but feral cats circle to protect him.

Darkness and day and a dog howling and the body free of its pain—you know not what you've done—and the fog of the night gone and the light touching your face and the white wings of birds once more and forever illuminated.

Blessed are you who hunger. Impossible as he seems, I did not invent the boy with the beatitudes inscribed on his body—a living text he is, thorns and doves, red slashes. *Blessed are you, pierced by mercy.* The tattooed boy comes to me three times in the days after, passes me on the street, not knowing.

Gabriel, my brother—

> one day we ran out in the rain
> just as the rain started—
> we lay down in the street,
> let the rain be the rain,
> warm drops then cold pellets—
> we stood shivering

in the rain
to see our bodies
bare on the street,
the dry places
we'd been, to know
our borders—we watched
our selves pocked
and filled with rain,
our selves gone,
our bodies
vanishing.

Inside we stripped
our clothes—so cold
we couldn't speak,
so cold
we took a bath together.

Tonight I lie awake in the rain and feel your breath, the rain, your heart inside me. Tonight while we lie dying in the rain, time spins backward, and the girl you killed is rising up, unwounded, so graceful we can't believe, a puppet with limp legs pulled by strings, strong but too fine to see, utterly transparent.

If she's scared of you, a jittery, jumpy boy in a raccoon mask and hooded sweatshirt—if she's nervous, if she smells adrenaline pumping off your body, if she's disgusted by your filth, she will not show it.

The homeless men drift in and out of the store every day, every hour, and she looks away while they fill their pockets with Mallomars and bags of peanuts. She says, I'm about to dump the coffee, make a new pot—take what's there if you want it—and they do—five creams, six sugars—and she loves them for their hunger—Emily Ryan, this girl who sings so beautifully in choir, whose clear soprano voice could surge and soar, but she holds the voice back, lets it rise and fall, lets it be with the others—baritone, tenor—not one alone, but one of many—lets the voices of all move through blood and bone, pelvis, sacrum—this girl who believes sound more than sense, the trembling body—who loves her body when she sings, this holy place, this vessel where the voices of men and the voices of women and through them the voice of God enter, where her voice is one and all and God is inside and everywhere around her, infinite God overfilling her body, and nothing is not God, not sound, not whole, not part of her.

Sometimes, when she sees the men, their raw skin, their sharp bones, she wants them to sing with her, to know love as sound, their own perfection.

The women scare her more, jittery reflections of herself, unnamed possibilities, Aunt Avila locked in the house by Uncle Jude, a bolt too high for her to reach—because she goes, because she wanders—because he finds her leaning to the water—but the girl wonders which comes first: the locked door, or a woman's madness.

Brother, time stops and starts and spins, and now it is the night before, and the girl lies on her bed, on the flowered quilt as old as she is, blue and green, rose and violet, each silk square stuffed and stitched (with all my love) *by Aunt Avila.*

Above her, a mobile strung with ninety-nine paper cranes swirls, faded birds folded by her mother, one a day for ninety-nine days, (waiting for you to come into the world). *Inside each bird, a single word, a prayer, moonlight and rain, written by her father.*

Brother, what we hear now is the absence of human voices. Pine,
wind, wolf, lily. We are unfolding the birds in the rain, letting
the rain be the rain, letting the rain tear them, letting the rain
wash the words:

----

we are making poems of the words

‒‒‒‒‒‒‒‒‒‒

‒‒‒‒‒‒‒

‒‒‒‒

‒‒‒‒‒‒‒‒‒

we will need no more words

ever

ACKNOWLEDGMENTS

I thank the Lannan Foundation for providing sanctuary in Marfa, Texas. I am also grateful to the John Simon Guggenheim Memorial Foundation; the National Endowment for the Arts; Corby Skinner and the Writer's Voice Project in Billings, Montana; Bob Goldberg and the Tanner Humanities Center; and the University of Utah. The faith of these individuals and the support of these institutions have made my work possible.

For their extraordinary contributions to research; their playful, healing presence; their enduring love and unwavering belief, I thank my family. Dear Gary, Glenna, Laurie, Wendy, Tom, Melinda, Nathan, Kelsey, Amanda, Chris, Mike, Brad, Alyssa, Hayley— dear Mom, our most marvelously surprising, radiant teacher—dear Father even now and always—Dear Cleora, Randy, Alicia, Kimmer, Kristi—Dear Jan and John: your wild love and beautiful lives are the light behind and within all stories.

To my students who bewilder and amaze me: Thank you.

By the companionship, love, insight and inspiration of my dear friends and early readers—Lance and Andi Olsen, Katharine Coles, Paisley Rekdal, Scott Black, Michael Mejia, Noy Holland, and Mary Pinard—I am endlessly and forever restored and blessed.

To Camie Schaefer, first responder, guardian angel: the grace and goodness of your being sustain me.

"The Bodies of Birds" appeared in *Image: A Journal of the Arts and Religion* in 2016.

Orion published a shorter version of "In the Exclusion Zone" in the March/April 2016 issue.

"Requiem in the Rain" and "In the Exclusion Zone" are composed from edited, rearranged, transformed selections originally published in *Silence & Song*. I am grateful to the editorial board of Fiction Collective Two, Dan Waterman, and the University of Alabama Press for permission to reprint these passages.

Numerous documentary, environmental, and historical sources informed and inspired "In the Exclusion Zone," most notably: *Voices from Chernobyl,* by Svetllana Alexievich; *Wormwood Forest,* by Mary Mycio; *Chernobyl: Confessions of a Reporter,* by Igor Kostin; *Radioactive Wolves* (PBS); and "Life in the Zone," by Steve Featherstone (*Harper's,* June 2011). I am grateful to the speakers, composers, and compilers of these texts.

Dennis Kirkland graciously granted permission to use his luminous photograph of Owyhee Picture Jasper as the cover. Bless you.

I thank Ander Monson and the staff at New Michigan Press for their kindness and expertise, their exquisite work on this book and their generously abundant work in the world.

MELANIE RAE THON's most recent books are *The 7th Man, Silence & Song, Lover,* and *The Good Samaritan Speaks.* She is also the author of the novels *The Voice of the River, Sweet Hearts, Meteors in August,* and *Iona Moon,* and the story collections *In This Light, Girls in the Grass,* and *First, Body.* She is a recipient of a Fellowship in Creative Arts from The John Simon Guggenheim Memorial Foundation, a Whiting Writer's Award, the Hopwood Award, two Fellowships from the National Endowment for the Arts, and a Writer's Residency from the Lannan Foundation. In 2009, she was Virgil C. Aldrich Fellow at the Tanner Humanities Center. Originally from Montana, Melanie now lives in Salt Lake City, where she teaches in the Creative Writing and Literature Programs at the University of Utah.

✤

COLOPHON

Text is set in a digital version of Jenson, designed by Robert Slimbach in 1996, and based on the work of punchcutter, printer, and publisher Nicolas Jenson. The titles here are in Futura.

✼

NEW MICHIGAN PRESS, based in Tucson, Arizona,
prints poetry and prose chapbooks, especially
work that transcends traditional genre. Together
with DIAGRAM, NMP sponsors a yearly chapbook
competition.

DIAGRAM, a journal of text, art, and schematic,
is published bimonthly at THEDIAGRAM.COM.
Periodic print anthologies are available from the New
Michigan Press at NEWMICHIGANPRESS.COM.

CPSIA information can be obtained
at www.ICGtesting.com
Printed in the USA
FFHW021126290519
52708781-58222FF